MUSINGS OF A
SOUL

JUDITH FRANKLIN

To order additional copies of this book, contact:
Xlibris
1-888-795-4274
www.Xlibris.com
Orders@Xlibris.com

ISBN: 978-1-7960-8866-3 (sc)
ISBN: 978-1-7960-8865-6 (e)

Print information available on the last page

Rev. date: 03/25/2020

MUSINGS OF A
SOUL

MUSINGS ON THE SEASHORE

BY JUDITH FRANKLIN

ON AN EARLY MORNING STROLL, DOWN A PRISTINE, AS YET
UNMARKED SEASHORE, BEFORE FOOT PRINTS, TIRE OR
OTHER MARKINGS COULD LEAVE THEIR IMPRINTS –
ONE CAN SEE AND DELIGHT IN FINDING TINY, FRAGILE
WHITE SHELLS, SAND DOLLARS, SMALL, DAINTY WHITE
FEATHERS, BITS OF SEAWEED, PIECES OF DRIFTWOOD-
ALL SOFTLY SERENADE THE NEW DAY –
YET. FROM THE HIGH HEAVENS, THE MASTER'S HANDS
HAD CRAFTED THESE TINY TREASURES, WITH THE SAME
POWER WITH WHICH HE HAD SPOKEN THE MIGHTY SEAS
INTO BEING; PLACED THE STARS IN THE HEAVENS, TO
GENTLY SPARKLE MAN'S DAY'S END, OR RECEIVE A
CHILD'S WHISPERED WISH; THE CLOUDS, SUN, MOON
AND PLANETS DANCE TO HIS COMMAND; MANKIND
WONDERS, IN AWE AT HOW WE ARE PROVIDED FOR,
WITH SUCH LOVE, AND HOW ALL CREATION
FILLS US WITH DELIGHT!

TWO GARDENS

TWO GARDENS, EACH SECLUDED, EACH BEAUTIFUL, EACH CHOSEN BY HIM, TO GRACE;
IN EVENING'S CLOAK, ONE, HE CHOSE, AND IN WHICH, HE KNELT, DEEP IN PRAYER,
SEEKING THE FATHER'S GRACE;
IN THE OTHER GARDEN, HE STOOD – RADIANT, JOYOUS –
HIS PURPOSE FULFILLED- HE HAD DESTROYED ALL SINNERS'
PLIGHT!
YES, THE LIGHT OF THE WORLD, ILLUMINED, FROM WITHIN,
TRULY OUTSHONE THE WORLD'S FIRST LIGHT –

TWO GARDENS

ON THAT HOLY SABBATH MORNING, WHILE ONLY ANGELS
SAW HIM, IN GLORY –
SLEEPING SINNERS KNEW NOT YET, HE HAD KEPT
THE PROMISE, COMPLETED NOW, WAS THE STORY ---
GOD HAD VISITED HIS PEOPLE, DRAWING THEM ONCE
MORE, UNTO HIMSELF –
TWO GARDENS, EACH EMBRACED HIM, ONE, IN ANGUISH
ONE IN VICTORY,
"..NO GREATER LOVE……

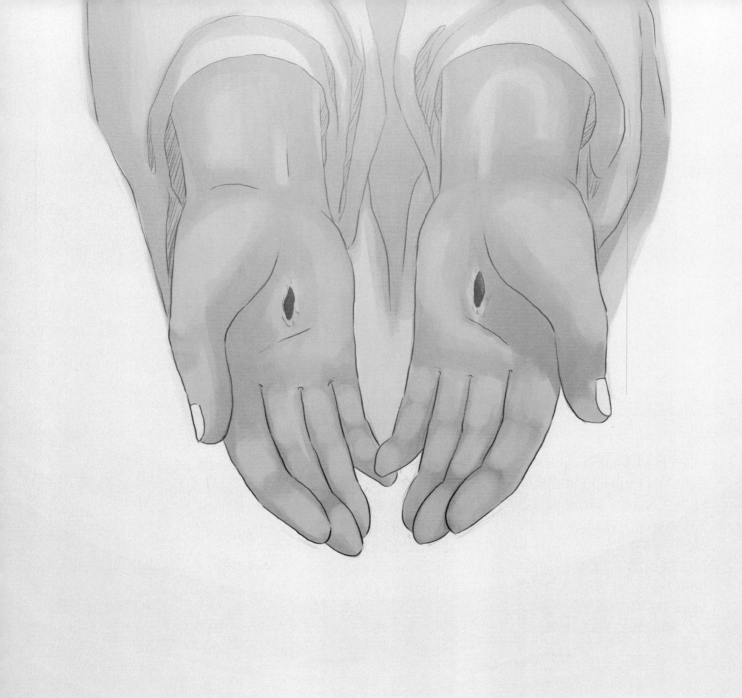

HANDS

THE HANDS THAT BLESSED THE CHILDREN;
THAT CALMED THE MIGHTY SEAS;
RAISED THE DEAD, CURED THE LEPERS;
HANDS THAT CHANGED WATER INTO WINE;
THAT WERE RAISED IN TEARFUL PRAYERS
OF SUPPLICATION, FOR ALL HIS PEOPLE;
HANDS THAT HEALED THE BLIND;
WERE ONE DAY PINIONED, WITH SPIKES,
TO A WOODEN CROSS OF TORTURE;
WHICH HORROR HIS LOVE BORE,
FOR SINNERS, FOR THOSE WHO,
HEARING HIS WORDS, SEEING HIS WORKS,
WOULD REPENT, THAT ONE GLORIOUS DAY-
HIS NAIL-SCARRED HANDS, WOULD RAISE UP
THOSE, HIS LAMBS, TO PARADISE, SET FREE!

WHERE, LORD ?

BY JUDITH FRANKLIN

<u>Where would you lead me today, Lord?</u> Shall I
walk past a homeless brother or sister?
Or, do I remember that might well be THEE?
Give me a generous heart, a non-judgmental mind,
so that I think to give to that poor soul a bottle of
cold water, or perhaps a banana? Shall I kindly ask
if he or she knows about a homeless shelter in this
city? Or, again- am I too preoccupied with my own
problems?
Do I, rather, in another setting, not notice the
harried mother with small children, in the check-out
counter, searching desperately in her purse for
change? Do I inwardly sigh, impatient, that she is
holding me up? Or, with compassion, as I see
her, embarrassed, having to put back some items
for which she cannot pay, smile at her cranky
children, tugging at her coat, begging for candy?
Without bravado, do I quietly give each one a candy,
Seemingly unaware of others waiting in line behind
Me? Then, do I see her look of gratitude, forgetting
Everyone and my own problems for a moment?
This is a golden opportunity to serve YOU, my LORD!
Do I, instead, think "how could someone be so dumb
not to plan ahead for how much money she had?"
How many times a day do we encounter YOU,
Master, in the faces and clothing of many of
Your people?
Lord, you ARE with us, all around us, in
the stranger, the prisoner, the homeless, the
disabled, the lonely, the forgotten, all of whom
might well stand, no longer in disguise, at
our individual Judgment?
<u>"WHATSOEVER YOU DID TO THESE, THE LEAST
OF MY BRETHREN, YOU DID IT TO ME!"</u>

JERUSALEM

BY JUDITH FRANKLIN

OH! JERUSALEM, HOW GREAT YOUR SHAME!
THOUGH UNWORTHY TO SPEAK HIS HOLY NAME;
YET, YOU CLAMORED FOR HIS DEATH,
AND WITH YOUR LOVE OF GORE;
SENTENCED HIM TO DEATH ON A CROSS –
WHICH HE SILENTLY BORE.
HIS TEARS FELL INTO THE DUST THAT DAY;
OBLIVIOUS, YOU MOCKED HIM, ALL THE WAY
TO GOLGOTHA, THE PLACE OF DEATH –
YOU DRAGGED YOUR SAVIOR AND YOUR GOD;
EVEN THEN, HIS BLOODY FOOTPRINTS
BLESSED THE GROUND HE TROD.
YOU STAND NOT ALONE, IN YOUR TRANSGRESSIONS
OF THAT DAY –
WE, TOO MOCKED AND SPAT UPON HIM,
WITH OUR SINS AND MORAL DECAY;
THE LAMB OF GOD, SPOTLESS, LOVINGLY,
BORE OUR SIN; YET HIS GREATEST ACT OF LOVE
WAS TAUNTED, IN THE EVIL, PAGAN DIN;
HIS BLOOD, TEARS AND DEATH – THE KINGDOM'S COIN,
THE SACRED GOD-MAN, IN ALL BUT SIN, DID OUR NATURE JOIN.
THE HANDS THAT HEALED, BLESSED, AND FOR US ALL PRAYED,
HUNG LIFELESS, ON A CROSS, OUR DEBT WAS PAID!
HE DID NOT HAVE TO ENDURE SUCH A TORTUOUS PLIGHT,
YET FREELY CHOSE TO FILL THE WORLD WITH HIS LIGHT!
NOW, THE LAMB SITS IN GLORY, VICTORIOUSLY, ON HIS THRONE;
AND, NOW – NOT ONE REPENTANT SINNER WALKS TO HIS DEATH ALONE.
LORD JESUS, SPOTLESS VICTIM, LAMB AND HIGH PRIEST –
YOU SUFFERED THE SENTENCE RESERVED FOR THE VERY LEAST!

ALLELUIA !!

SONG OF A SOUL

BY JUDITH FRANKLIN

CREATED BY THE BREATH OF GOD, TO LIVE
ETERNALLY,
TO SHINE, SING TO HIM, THE CREATOR,
AND MEANT TO ENTER INTO HIS KINGDOM,
AT LIFE'S END—IF EACH CREATURE FOLLOWED
HIS COMMANDS;
MY BEAUTY, IF YOU COULD SEE ME, EXCEEDS
MORTAL MAN'S IMAGINATION! WHY WOULDN'T I?
HIS SACRED HANDS FORMED ME.
MANY MAGNIFICENT MANSIONS, ONE FOR EACH
CREATURE HE CREATED, WHO FOLLOW HIM;
IF EACH OF YOU, MANKIND, COULD SEE IT,
YOU WOULD SURELY FAINT!
YOUR GUARDIAN ANGEL, EVER BESIDE YOU,
GUARDS YOU FROM THE DANGERS WHICH ARE
TRAPS LAID BY EVIL, WHICH "PRINCE OF THIS
WORLD" WANTS YOU TO INDULGE IN, THEREBY
RISKING YOUR INTENDED CELESTIAL DWELLING!
YOUR ANGEL WHISPERS TO YOU WHEN
TEMPTATIONS ARISE. HEED HIM, FOR THE
TREASURES ABOVE! DO NOT WANDER FROM
THE PATH OF RIGHTEOUSNESS;
YOUR ANGEL WEEPS, BITTERLY, SHOULD YOU
FALL. GRACE ABOUNDS, FOR YOU TO CALL
ON, IN REPENTANCE, FOR YOU ARE A CHILD
OF THE LIGHT! A TRUE CHILD OF GOD!
I LONG FOR THE DAY IN WHICH YOU RECEIVE
YOUR CALLING. THEN, AT LAST, YOU WILL
SEE THE KING OF KINGS! BE STRONG, WALK
IN HIS PEACE AND GRACE, THAT YOU MIGHT
HEAR: "WELL DONE, GOOD AND FAITHFUL
SERVANT! ENTER INTO MY KINGDOM, PREPARED
FOR THOSE WHO LOVE ME!"

GOD'S SKYLIGHT

BY JUDITH FRANKLIN

HE LOOKS DOWN, WITH DELIGHT, AT HIS
HANDIWORK: TREES, ALL TYPES, GREENERY,
THERE WERE HIS SEVEN, ROARING SEAS,
TEEMING WITH A PLETHORA OF CREATURES,
OF ALL TYPES, SIZES, SHAPES; THE SYMPHONY
OF COLORS OF FLOWERS, BLOOMS SO RADIANT
THEY SEEMED TO DANCE; THEN- AS IF A CELESTIAL
TRUMPET ANNOUNCED TO CREATION HIS
"CROWN JEWELS" – HIS MAJESTIC MOUNTAINS!
THEY STOOD PROUD, SOME SOARING
SO HIGH, AS IF TO BE HIS FOOT STOOL; HIS
PHENOMENAL WORK CONTINUED ITS DISPLAY,
IN HIS MANY SPECIES OF CREATURES,
DIFFERING IN SIZE, SHAPE, OTHERS SWAM,
SOME WALKED UPRIGHT, WHILE SOME CRAWLED;
MANY TO BE FOOD, SOME FOR COMPANIONSHIP,
THESE FOR HUMANS, HIS FINAL CREATION.
HOW JOYOUSLY HE HAD HUNG THE STARS, TO
ADORN THE NIGHT SKIES, TO DELIGHT MAN!
<u>ALL OF IT GOOD!!</u>
<u>WHAT TYPE OF STEWARDS HAS MANKIND BEEN?</u>

FATHER

BY JUDITH FRANKLIN

I HAVE: LOVE FOR YOU;
                  SORROW FOR MY SINS;
                  NEED OF YOUR AID;
                  HOPE FOR MY SALVATION;
                  JOY IN YOUR CREATION;

I HAVE: STRENGTH WITH YOUR PROTECTION;
                  FERVOR WITH YOUR GRACE;
                  COURAGE WITH YOUR MIGHT;
                  COMPASSION WITH YOUR HEART;
                      AND:

                  I WILL HAVE ETERNAL LIFE, WITH YOUR MERCY!!

CRY OF THE LAMB

BY JUDITH FRANKLIN

COME DOWN, PRECIOUS LORD, TO THIS, THY LAMB,
LIFT ME, SOOTHE ME, WITH THY SHEPHERD'S TOUCH;
I WANDERED, IN MY FOOLISHNESS, AND LOST MY WAY;
I NEED THY STAFF, TO GUIDE ME.
YOU CALL, AND LOOK – NEVER CEASING, LEAVING THE
OTHERS, FOR YOU KNOW EACH OF YOUR LAMBS, AND
WE FOLLOW;
THIS ONE OF YOUR LAMBS, FOR WHICH YOU SEARCH,
LONGS FOR YOU;
I NEED YOUR SOOTHING BALM, YOUR TENDER TOUCH-
GOOD SHEPHERD, COME, HOIST ME UPON YOUR SHOULDERS;
I SHALL STRAY NEVER MORE, HEAR THOU MY CRY;
COME, RESCUE ME, AND CARRY ME HOME!

WITH THY LOVE IN MY HEART

BY JUDITH FRANKLIN

WITH THY LOVE IN MY HEART, THY GRACE IN MY SOUL;
MY TRUST IN THY MERCY AND COMPASSION,
THY STRENGTH MAKES ME WHOLE;
OH LORD! HOW I LONG TO SEE THY GLORIOUS FACE!
HOW I ACHE, MASTER, FOR THY WONDROUS EMBRACE!
GRANT ME, LORD, THE STRENGTH TO FINISH THE RACE!
IN THEE, ALONE, MY TRUST I PLACE;
THE STONES, THE NAILS, THE REBUKE YOU BORE –
THE AGONY, THE BITTER CUP, YOU DRANK IT ALL –
THAT WE MIGHT LIVE, FOREVER MORE !!

TEARS IN THE HEART

BY JUDITH FRANKLIN

They are many: soothing, or, borne of sorrow;
Swiftly springing from the chambers of the soul;
Our many changing emotions bring these tears;
While invisible to others, yet mercifully transparent;
To the Creator, Who witnesses and counts them;
HE knew we would need a private shelter,
For powerful feelings, which would remain our own;
HE told us not one hair falls from our heads, that escape
HIS eyes; even lilies in the field are arrayed by HIS Hands.
Wondrously made, we humans have powers, systems,
Outlets, for releasing feelings, raising Psalms of praise-
To His Majesty, with hearts big enough to love mightily!

SANDS ON THE SHORE

BY JUDITH FRANKLIN

WE, THE MILLIONS, ARE AS SANDS ON HIS OWN SEASHORE;
HE STROLLS GENTLY, UPON THE SHORELINE, TREASURING
EACH SEEMINGLY TINY GRAIN, TENDERLY VIEWING EACH ONE;
AS THE LAPPING WAVES WASH UP, NO DESTRUCTION OCCURS –
RATHER – EACH ONE IS A BLESSING, CORRECTION OR GENTLE
CHALLENGE, DEPENDING UPON THE MASTER'S DIRECTION OR
PERMISSION, AS THE STORMS GATHER OR, SUBSIDE;
THOUGH TO THE EYES OF THE BEHOLDER, EACH TINY GRAIN
HAS NO SPECIAL WORTH – YET TO HIM, THE CREATOR –
EACH MINUTE PARTICLE FORMS TO A BEAUTIFUL SYMPHONY,
PLEASING TO HIM, FORMING A CELESTIAL CREATION,
ONLY HE CAN HEAR!!

Printed in the United States
By Bookmasters